ISBN: 9781659872842
Printed in the United States of America
First Printing, 2020

Conrad FE Media
@conradfemedia
conradfemedia@photographer.net

BUT SPHERE ITSELF

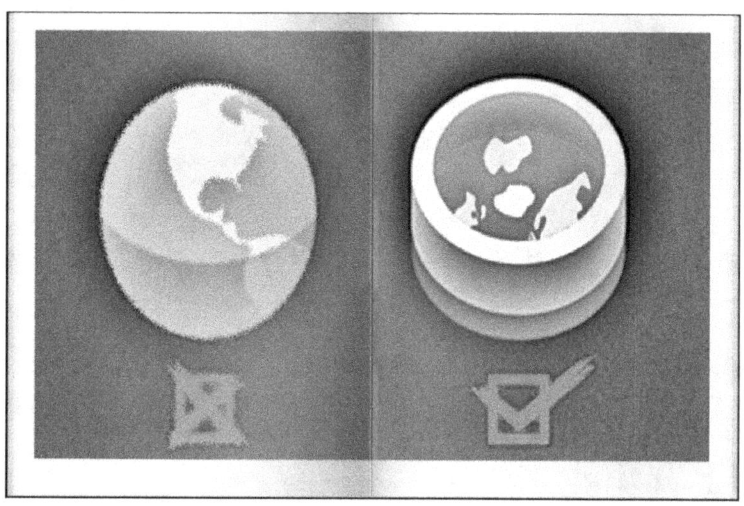

A Flat Earth Theory
Research Reference Guide

by Christopher Conrad

So the movement has finally piqued your curiosity, huh?

Wouldn't it be nice to have a head start on your flat earth research?

Suppose there is a Facebook group for people thinking the moon is made out of green cheese. Would you "waste your time" joining a group like that to discuss the subject and find arguments against it, if you are 100% certain that the Earth is not made of cheese?

Then why are "globeheads" JOINING flat earth groups in droves??

To FIGHT (and some of them get REEEAAAALLLYYY mad!!!!) against such a ludicrous idea?

Or are they afraid
something will come out
to shake up their
understanding of reality?

I say there is nothing to
fear, "but sphere itself",
hence the title of this
book.

Deep down you know it,
but you don't remember.
That's not your fault, but

refusing to relearn it is no one's fault but yours because you can do quite simple experiments that will prove beyond a shadow of a doubt that, while the Earth may not in fact be "flat", it most certainly can NOT be a globe, or a pear/orange/apple shaped planet hurdling through space at unimaginable speeds while this theory "thing" we call gravity keeps the oceans from slinging off like water would from a wet spinning tennis ball.

The only people who don't know the Earth can't POSSIBLY be a globe are those too uninterested or too busy to do a proper and complete investigation of the matter.

COUNTLESS experiments

have been and are being done by scientists and laymen alike all over the world (EVEN KIDS!) as I write this. I'm sorry to say that full disclosure of "non-globular earth" is going to mess some people up pretty bad (maybe more so than when other-dimensional or otherworldly beings are FULLY disclosed in the near future. Soft disclosure has been going on for a while now.)....those who refuse to or aren't able to evolve, adapt and even embrace new ideas, standards and sciences....a new paradigm.

Boundaries are only there to be crossed.

Trust me that I'm very well aware that many people who care about me and many who may have never even met me are reading this right now and thinking, "This guy MUST be a straight up LUNATIC or something? How can anyone who's educated himself as much as Christopher Conrad claims to have, say something as stupid as the Earth isn't spherical?" (You're thinking something like that as you read this sentence, right? Lol)

Well, it's quite simple. I heard about the theory decades ago and for twenty years never gave it ONE THOUGHT because of how absolutely ridiculous of an idea it was. I remember thinking how can such smart and educated people waste so much time on utter "BULLSHIT"? I was offended and frankly kind of upset that so many trees were cut down to make books about such an obviously untrue notion, and made up my mind that I wouldn't waste **ONE MINUTE** of my precious life devoted to such idiocy. I made a decision that many of you are making right now. I clung to my beliefs and went about my life, never giving it another thought **EVER** for over 20 years.

For years I went through life experiences while gorging on countless books on every subject that piqued my interest, won accolades chasing my dreams, got married a couple times, had kids, been incarcerated, met Lady Ayahuasca, and basically evolved a lot over the years until one day I came across it again. This time, though, it was from a very trusted source, and I thought, there **HAS** to be something to it. I dug in!

Honestly, it didn't take long at all for me to realize that I made a **HUGE** mistake not digging into this earlier. I'll leave it at that. If you don't **SERIOUSLY** look at the evidence being presented by **COUNTLESS** people worldwide, then you will never know. You won't get it from TV, or Hollywood or religion or anywhere other than researching on your own. Don't take my or ANYone's word for it, analyze the evidence and make sure you're not mistaking assumptions as fact. Assumptions ARE NOT facts.

The math is the key.

All you have to do is the

math. The math won't lie to you. It can't lie to you. The math is the one proof that we have which allows us to KNOW beyond a shadow of a doubt. The math is there, the ball (no pun intended lol) is in your court.

Following are some of the most conclusive writings on the subject (available completely free of charge) and no one should "make up there mind" on whether they "believe" the Earth to be flat or spherical without examining the evidence.

A doctor wouldn't diagnose you with cancer and prescribe destructive chemotherapy without first running a myriad of tests to make sure he wasn't giving an invasive treatment to someone who didn't need it, right?

A thorough examination is necessary, so give the evidence presented in this reference book a thorough examination before proclaiming your ignorance on the matter to the world.

Once you have examined all the available evidence you will be much more of an expert on the subject than the millions of people attempting to debunk Flat Earth Theory with little to zero actual research having been done by them.

This first list is made up of PDF hyperlinked public domain works conveniently archived for your personal reference as you embark on this journey of discovery.

["Earth Not A Globe! An Experimental Inquiry into](

the True Figure of the Earth" Samuel Rowbotham "Foundations of Many Generations" by E. Eschini

"Is Newtonian Astronomy True?" by William Carpenter

"Kings Dethroned" by Gerard Hickson

"The Midnight Sun" by Albert Smith

"The Sea-Earth Globe and and its Monstrous Hypothetical Motions" by

Albert Smith
"Museum of Science and Art (Vol. 1)" by Dionysius Lardner
"Zetetic Astronomy" by Lady Blount, Albert Smith
"The Enlightenment of the World" by John G. Abizaid

There are many more books on the subject that aren't in the public domain and some other pertinent collections. Here are a few I would recommend:

["Adrian Galilio" by Lady Blount](#)
["Foundations of Many Generations " by E. Eschini](#)
["Can You Speak Venusian?" (excerpt) by Sir Patrick Moore](#)
["Eccentric Lives and Peculiar Notions" by John Michell](#)

"Eccentric Lives and Peculiar Notions" (excerpt) by John Mitchell

"Heaven and Flat Earth" by Gabrielle Henriete

"The Square Pegs: Americans Who Dared to be Different" by Irving Wallace

"The New Madrid Earthquake 1812" by Myron L. Fuller

The Phoenician Origins of Britons, Scots and Anglo-Saxons

The Travels of Marco Polo the Venetian

Book of the Damned by Charles Fort

Atlantis Book Collection

An Ottoman Mentality: The World of Evliya Çelebi

THE KOLBRIN BIBLE PDF + ULTIMATE RESOURCE PAGE

The Chronology of Ancient Kingdoms Amended

Orbits of Ancient and Medieval Comets by Ichiro Hasegawa

<u>Natural Magic 1669</u>
<u>The Sacred Theory of the Earth by Thomas Burnet</u>
<u>The Sacred Theory of the Earth Vol II by Thomas Burnet</u>
<u>Etidorpha</u>

Some galleries and libraries that are be mandatory stops on the road to the most complete understanding of Flat Earth Theory would be:

Bildarchiv der Bayerischen Staatsbibliothek

Ketterer Kunst

Astrophysics Data System -Harvard

World Digital Library

Oxford Libraries

e-rara Swiss Library

Ancient Origins

Digitale-Sammlungen

Shorpy

Internet Archive Library

Gallica

Vatican Library
DONum- University of Liege
Wellcome Collection
British Library Online
NYPL Digital Collections
Babel Hathi Trust
Smithsonian Libraries
Tart-Aria Info
Bilderbuch-Berlin
J. Paul Getty Museum

Some maps you might want to inspect and reference along this

journey of geographical education are:

[9 Extremely Ancient Maps That Should Not Exist](#)
[World Landbridge](#)
[Library of Congress Geography and Maps](#)
[Old Maps Online](#)
[Birds Eye Views](#)
[Götzfried Antique Maps](#)
[Mappa Mundi](#)
[David Rumsey Map Collection](#)
[Raremaps.com](#)

<u>Wikipedia Early World Maps</u>
<u>Altea Gallery World Maps</u>

I'll leave it up to you and your research to figure out where to go from here after you analyze the evidence contained herein.

I'd like to note one thing before I conclude this

reference book. Today's
most prominent quantum
physicists as well as
many spirutual leaders
and gurus the world over,
all concur that what we
call reality, this matrix,
this conglomeration of
consciousness is in all
actuality a field of
computer code with
infinite possibility that
can "become" whatever
each and every
consciousness manifests it

to be. Well, in so many words. If this is to be believed, then it is, in effect, possible for the Earth to be sphericle AND flat. But this would be another book entirely so I'll leave you with that and bless you on your search for higher consciounsess.

Good luck and may the Source be with you.

If you appreciate the information shared here and would like to tune in to the weekly podcast the author hosts concerning higher consciousness, please tune in to The THC Show at http://www.thethcshow.com

Namaste

THAT MOMENT WHEN YOU UNDERSTAND THAT THEY WERE GOING TO ASSAULT THE FIRMAMENT...
THEY KNEW ABOUT GATES IN THE FIRMAMENT, THAT WERE USED TO FLOOD THE EARTH.

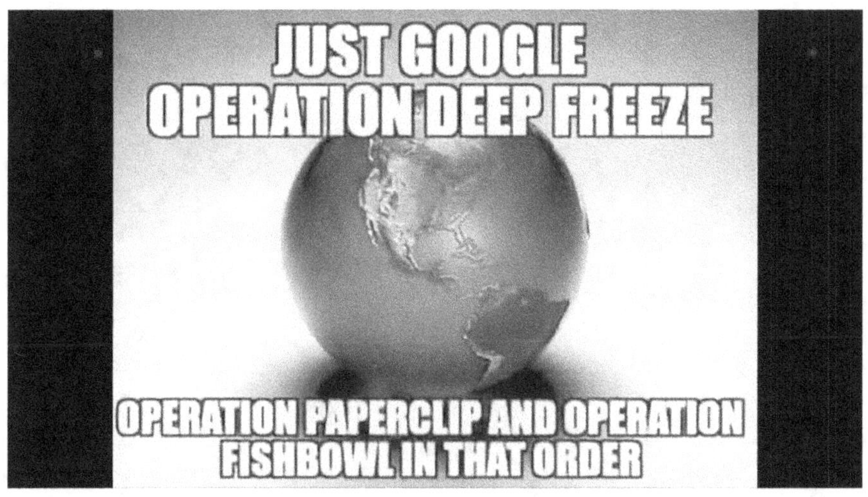
JUST GOOGLE OPERATION DEEP FREEZE
OPERATION PAPERCLIP AND OPERATION FISHBOWL IN THAT ORDER

RESEARCH FLAT EARTH!